# A Young Pianist's
# FIRST HYMNAL

Favorite Hymns arranged for Piano Solo with Optional Duet Accompaniments

## BY WILLIAM GILLOCK

ISBN 978-1-5400-4002-2

WILLIS MUSIC

EXCLUSIVELY DISTRIBUTED BY

**HAL•LEONARD®**
7777 W. BLUEMOUND RD. P.O. BOX 13819
MILWAUKEE, WISCONSIN 53213

© 1976 by The Willis Music Co.
International Copyright Secured  All Rights Reserved

Visit Hal Leonard Online at
**www.halleonard.com**

Contact us:
**Hal Leonard**
7777 West Bluemound Road
Milwaukee, WI 53213
Email: info@halleonard.com

In Europe, contact:
**Hal Leonard Europe Limited**
42 Wigmore Street
Marylebone, London, W1U 2RN
Email: info@halleonardeurope.com

In Australia, contact:
**Hal Leonard Australia Pty. Ltd.**
4 Lentara Court
Cheltenham, Victoria, 3192 Australia
Email: info@halleonard.com.au

# CONTENTS

# Doxology

From PSALM C

Melody from GENEVA PSALTER

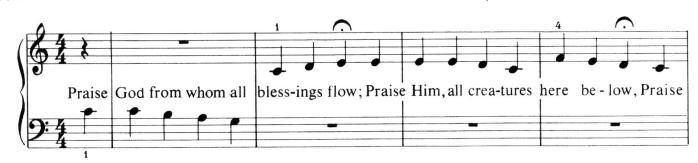

Praise | God from whom all | bless-ings flow; Praise Him, all crea-tures here be - low, Praise

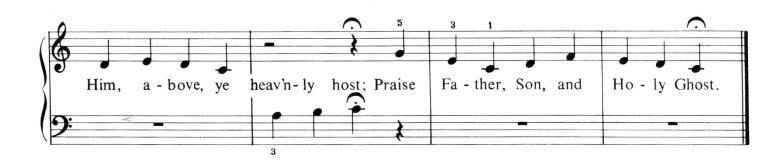

Him, a - bove, ye heav'n-ly host; Praise | Fa - ther, Son, and | Ho - ly Ghost.

# Doxology
(Duet Accompaniment)

# Jesus Loves Me

(Duet Accompaniment)

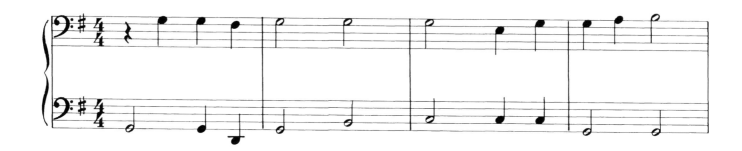

# Jesus Loves Me

Anna B. Warner

William B. Bradbury

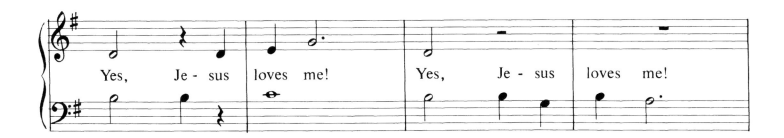

# Faith Of Our Fathers

(Duet Accompaniment)

# Faith Of Our Fathers

Frederick W. Faber

Henry F. Hemy

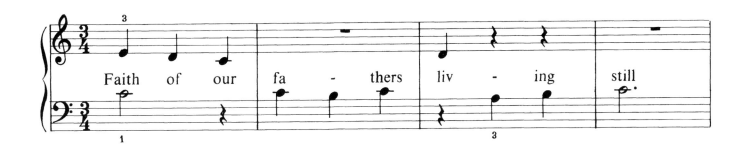

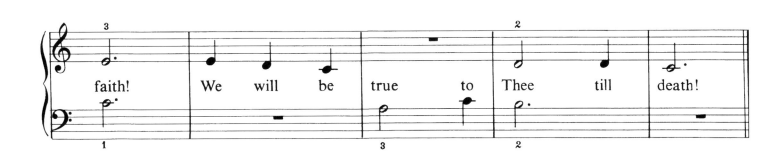

# Abide With Me

(Duet Accompaniment)

# Abide With Me

Henry Francis Lyte

William Henry Monk

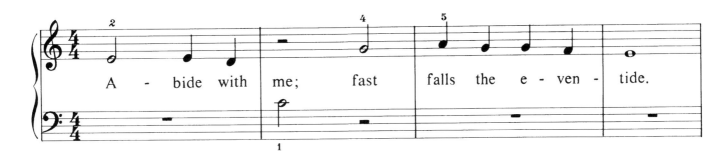

A - bide with me; fast falls the e - ven - tide.

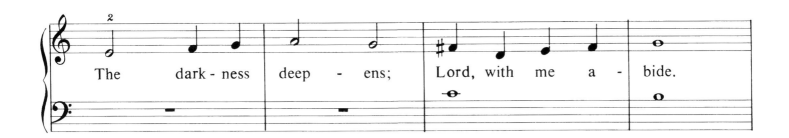

The dark - ness deep - ens; Lord, with me a - bide.

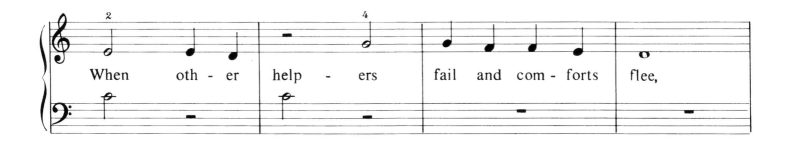

When oth - er help - ers fail and com - forts flee,

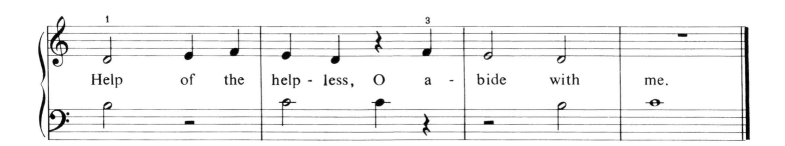

Help of the help - less, O a - bide with me.

# Holy Holy Holy!

(Duet Accompaniment)

# Holy, Holy, Holy !

Reginald Heber

John B. Dykes

Ho - ly, ho - ly, ho - ly! Lord God Al - might - y!

Ear - ly in the morn - ing our song shall rise to Thee.

Ho - ly, ho - ly, ho - ly! Mer - ci - ful and might - y,

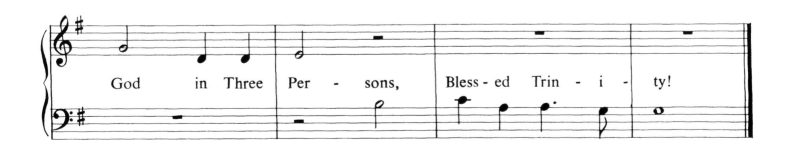

God in Three Per - sons, Bless - ed Trin - i - ty!

# For The Beauty Of The Earth

(Duet Accompaniment)

# For The Beauty Of The Earth

Folliott S. Pierpoint

Conrad Kocher

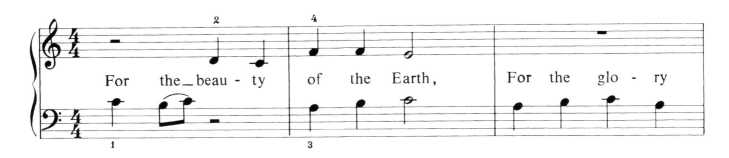

For the beau - ty of the Earth, For the glo - ry

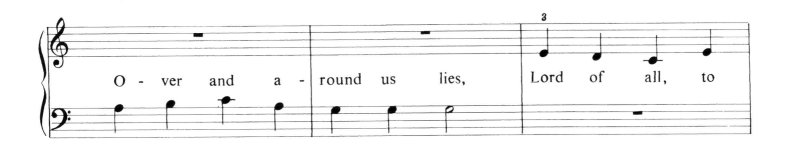

of the skies, For the love which from our birth

O - ver and a - round us lies, Lord of all, to

Thee we raise This our hymn of grate - ful praise.

# Sweet Hour Of Prayer

(Duet Accompaniment)

# Sweet Hour Of Prayer

W. W. Walford

William B. Bradbury

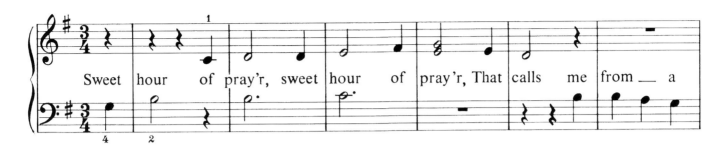

Sweet hour of pray'r, sweet hour of pray'r, That calls me from ___ a

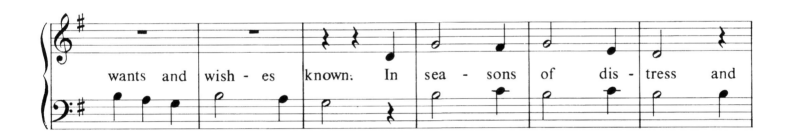

World of care, And bids me to my Fa - ther's throne, Make all my

wants and wish - es known; In sea - sons of dis - tress and

grief, My soul has of - ten found re - lief, And oft es -

caped the temp - ter's snare By thy re - turn, ___ sweet hour of pray'r.

# My Faith Looks Up To Thee

(Duet Accompaniment)

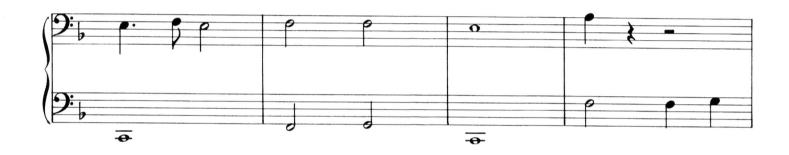

# My Faith Looks Up To Thee

Ray Palmer

Lowell Mason

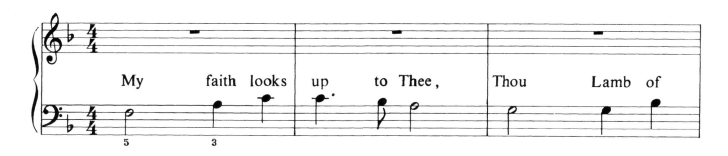

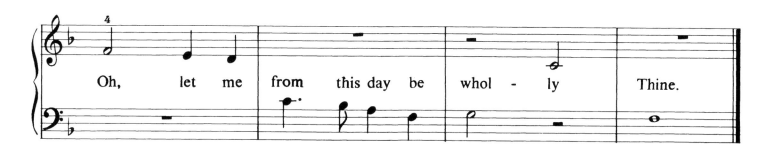

# Come, Thou Almighty King

(Duet Accompaniment)

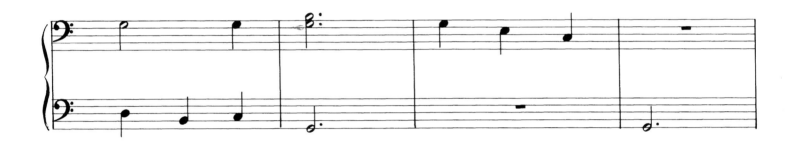

# Come, Thou Almighty King

Anonymous

Felice de Giardini

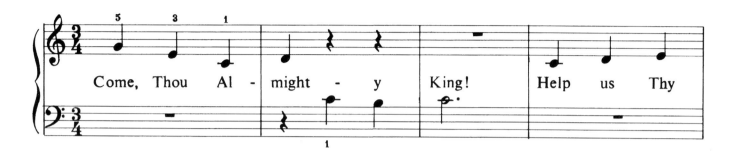

Come, Thou Al - might - y King! Help us Thy

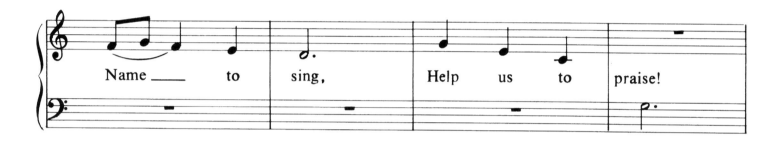

Name ___ to sing, Help us to praise!

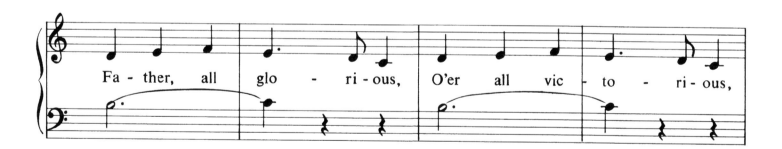

Fa - ther, all glo - ri - ous, O'er all vic - to - ri - ous,

Come and reign o - ver us, An - cient of Days.

# Fairest Lord Jesus

(Duet Accompaniment)

# Fairest Lord Jesus

Crusaders' Hymn

Anonymous

Silesian Folk Melody

# God Of Our Fathers

(Duet Accompaniment)

# God Of Our Fathers

National Hymn

Daniel C. Roberts

George W. Warren

Trumpets—optional

God of our fa - thers,

Whose al - might - y hand    Leads forth in beau - ty

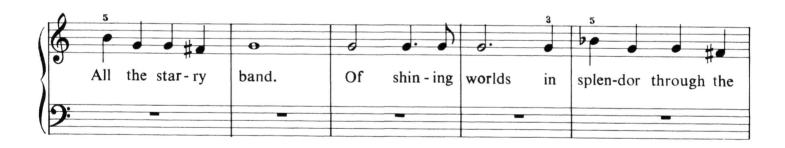

All the star - ry band.    Of shin - ing worlds in splen-dor through the

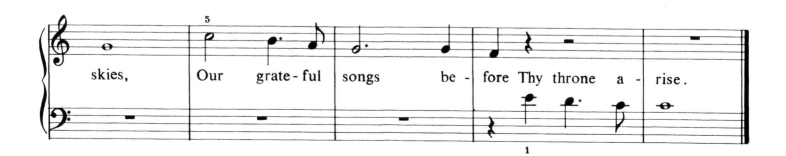

skies,    Our grate - ful songs    be - fore Thy throne a - rise.

# Softly Now The Light Of Day

(Duet Accompaniment)

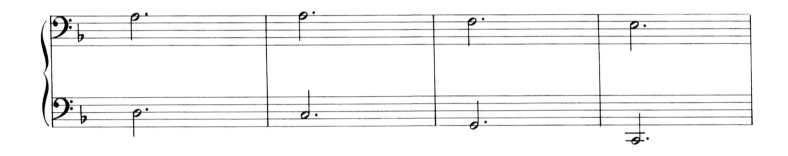

# Softly Now The Light Of Day

George W. Doane

Louis Moreau Gottschalk

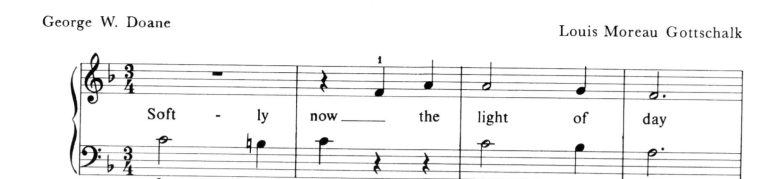

Soft - ly now ____ the light of day

Fades up - on ____ our sights a - way;

Free from care ____ and la - bor ____ free,

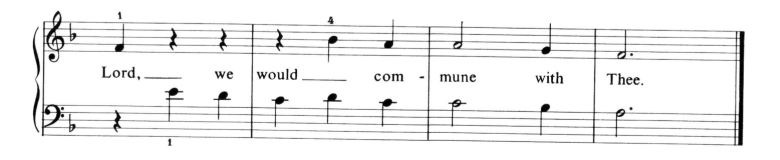

Lord, ____ we would ____ com - mune with Thee.

# Rock Of Ages

(Duet Accompaniment)

# Rock Of Ages

Augustus M. Toplady

Thomas Hastings

Rock of a - ges, cleft for me, Let me hide my-self in

thee; Let the wa - ter and the blood, From thy

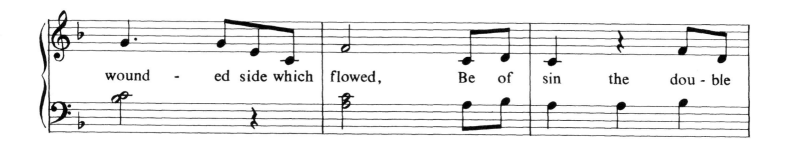

wound - ed side which flowed, Be of sin the dou - ble

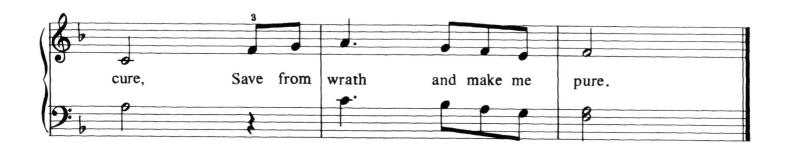

cure, Save from wrath and make me pure.

# Onward, Christian Soldiers

(Duet Accompaniment)

# Onward, Christian Soldiers

Sabine Baring—Gould

Arthur S. Sullivan

# Battle Hymn Of The Republic

(Duet Accompaniment)

# Battle Hymn Of The Republic

Julia Ward Howe

American Folk Melody

Mine eyes have seen the glo - ry of the com-ing of the Lord; He is

tram-pling out the vin - tage where the grapes of wrath are stored; He hath loosed the fate - ful

Light-ning of His ter - ri-ble swift sword, His truth is march - ing

on. _____ Glo - ry, glo - ry Hal - le - lu - jah! _____

Glo - ry, glo - ry, Hal - le - lu - jah! ___ Glo - ry, glo - ry, Hal - le -

lu - jah! Our God is march - ing on. _____

# Joyful, Joyful, We Adore Thee

Henry van Dyke

Ludwig van Beethoven

Joy - ful, joy - ful, we a - dore Thee, God of glo - ry, Lord of love;

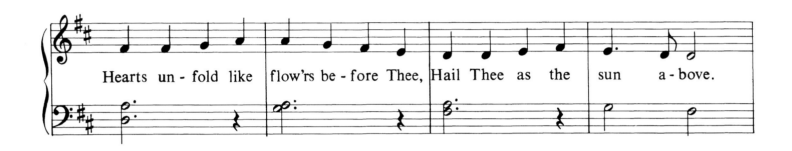

Hearts un - fold like flow'rs be - fore Thee, Hail Thee as the sun a - bove.

Melt the clouds of sin and sad - ness; Drive the dark of doubt a - way;

Giv - er of im - mor - tal glad - ness, Fill us with the light of day.